CONTENTS

INTRODUCTION

WHERE IS SPAIN?

Spain is in Europe, with France to the north-west. Spain and Portugal make a **peninsula**, which is surrounded by three seas: the Atlantic Ocean, the Bay of Biscay and the Mediterranean. The capital city of Spain is Madrid, where about 3 million people live.

This tower, in the city of Seville, was built about 1000 years ago. People say the first builders covered it in a layer of gold.

A cathedral in Santiago de Compostela. Spain has many grand cathedrals.

San Sebastian

Bilbao

ANDORRA

Valladolid

Barcelona

Zaragoza

Salamanca

● MADRID

Minorca

Palma de
Majorca

PORTUGAL

SPAIN

Valencia

Majorca

Ibiza

Alicante

Murcia

Seville

Almería

Malaga

AFRICA

City Population

○ over 1,000,000

● over 100,000

● capital

0   200 km

CANARY ISLANDS

Lanzarote

Tenerife   Fuerteventura

Las Palmas

Gran
Canaria

0   200 km

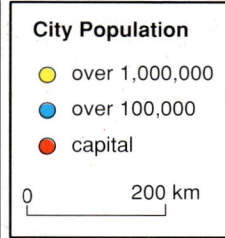

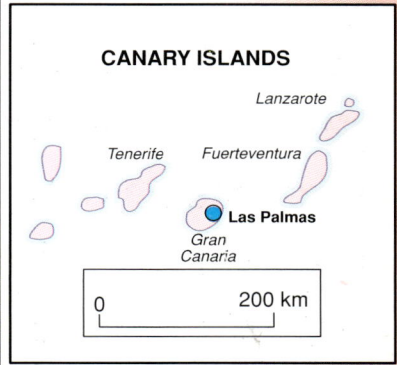

SPAIN'S HISTORY

Spain was part of the **Roman Empire** for about 600 years. In AD711 Muslim Arabs, called Moors, captured Spain. It split into different kingdoms, which often fought. In 1492 Spain became one country again, ruled by a king.

In 1930 there was a **civil war** in Spain. When the war ended, in 1939, the king had lost. But in 1975 the Spanish people decided to have a king again. Now the king rules with a **government** chosen by the people.

Because Spain used to be lots of different countries, there are still parts of Spain that have their own languages and traditions. Some people in these places would like to become separate from Spain again.

5

THE LAND

PLATEAU AND MOUNTAINS

Most of Spain is high, fairly flat land – a plateau. The plateau is not all flat. It is split into two by mountains. Rivers flow across the plateau, making valleys. Some valleys have rich soil and are good for farming. The smaller rivers sometimes dry up in the summer.

Spain is separated from France by the Pyrenees mountains.

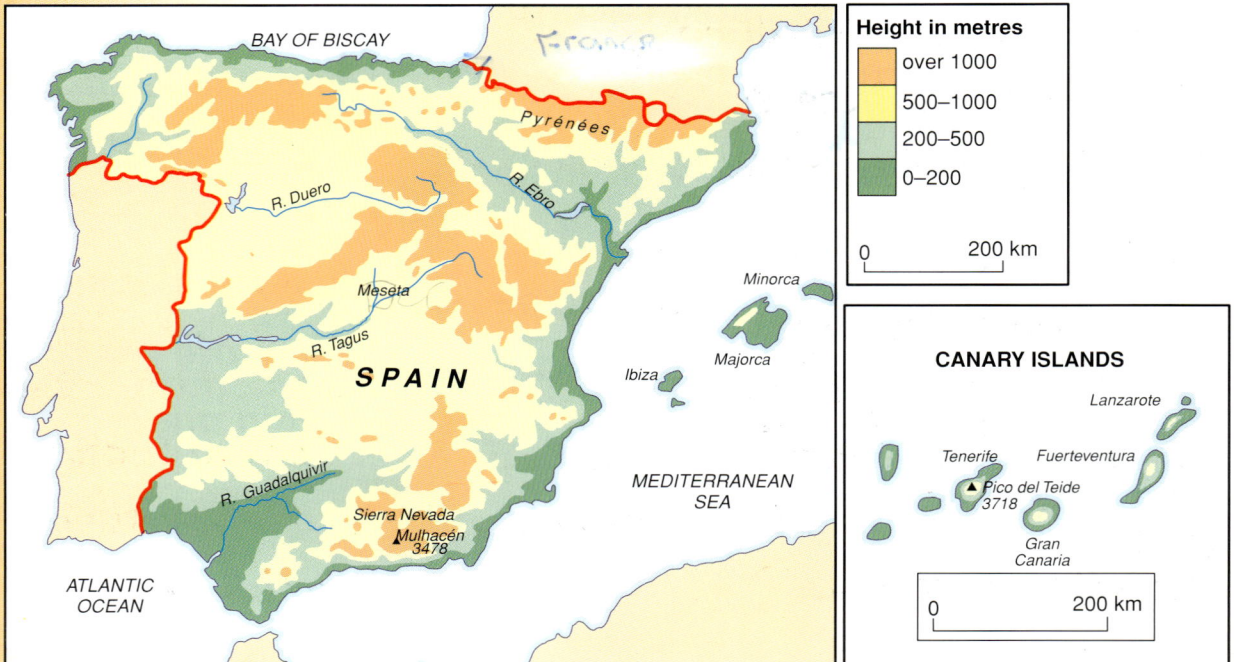

Height in metres	
	over 1000
	500–1000
	200–500
	0–200

BAY OF BISCAY

France

Pyrénées

R. Duero

R. Ebro

Meseta

R. Tagus

S P A I N

R. Guadalquivir

Sierra Nevada
Mulhacén
3478

ATLANTIC
OCEAN

Minorca

Majorca

Ibiza

MEDITERRANEAN
SEA

0   200 km

CANARY ISLANDS

Lanzarote

Tenerife   Fuerteventura

Pico del Teide
3718

Gran
Canaria

0   200 km

A volcano on Tenerife, in the Canary Islands. It has not erupted for a long time.

These windmills were once used to grind flour or to pump water up from under the ground.

SPAIN'S ISLANDS

Spain owns several islands off its coast, as well as the Canary Islands, off the coast of north-west Africa. Lots of **tourists** go to these islands on holiday, as well as going to Spain itself.

Most of the Canary Islands are old **volcanoes**. The sand on some of the beaches is black, because it is old **lava** from the volcanoes, worn down by the sea. These islands are hot and dry all year round.

Canary birds are named after the Canary Islands. They live there in the wild.

7

WEATHER, PLANTS AND ANIMALS

The Costa del Sol (Sunshine Coast), on Spain's Mediterranean coast, has lots of hotels for **tourists**, who come for the good weather.

THE WEATHER

On the plateau, winters are very cold and summers are very hot. On the Atlantic **coast** and in the north of Spain it is wetter and cooler than on the plateau. The weather on the Mediterranean coast is somewhere between the two.

PLANTS AND ANIMALS

The plants in Spain are different in different places. Trees grow in the cool, wet mountains and the north. In the hot dry areas, only a few bushes and grass grow. These areas are called scrubland.

There are not many wild animals left in Spain. Some of them, like bears, wolves, wild cats and wild boar are protected in **national parks**. Tarantula spiders are protected too!

You could go to prison if you harm animals in any of Spain's five national parks.

The town of Alicante has scrubland all around. A few orange and lemon trees grow there, too.

TOWNS AND CITIES

A **plaza** in the town of Caparossa. You can find squares like this in most Spanish towns and villages.

OLD TOWNS

Many of the towns and cities in Spain are very old. Some of them have walls built in the time of the **Roman Empire**.

There are lots of different buildings in the towns. They show how long the town has been lived in and what kinds of people lived there. Lots of towns and villages have buildings built by the Moors (like the Great Mosque in Cordoba) and also by the people who came after them.

Alicante, in southern Spain, has grown from a small town into a tourist resort.

Barcelona has grown outside its city walls. It is a busy port, a tourist resort and has lots of factories, too.

NEW BUILDING

Many old cities have grown outside their city walls. The old town centres are still very busy though. Lots of these towns are visited by **tourists** on holiday.

Tourists also go to the **coast**, especially on the islands and the Mediterranean coast. There are lots of new hotels, night-clubs and restaurants here, to attract the tourists.

LIVING IN VALENCIA

THE GRIJALVO FAMILY

Manuel and Cati Grijalvo live in a flat in the city of Valencia. They have one boy, Manu (who is twelve) and one girl, Begoña (who is ten).

The family live in a flat about half an hour's drive from the city centre.

THE FAMILY'S DAY

Manuel and Cati work full-time. Cati works in an office at the university. Manuel works for a book publisher. They each have a car to get around easily. Manu and Begoña both go to the same school.

Manu plays football for the Serranos Football Club.

Begoña goes to ballet lessons after school.

MEAL TIMES

The family can do their food shopping in the small shops near the flat. There are lots of shops.

The family are up early, at 6.30 am. They only have a small breakfast of coffee or hot chocolate and biscuits. They have lunch at work or school.

The family eat their main meal at about 7 pm. Manuel does not eat with them in the week. He often works late.

One of Cati's local shops. 'Frutas y Verduras' means 'Fruit and Vegetables'.

The family at breakfast.

13

FARMING IN SPAIN

Farmland in north-east Spain. Wheat is growing in the fields.

DIFFERENT CROPS

The farmers in Spain grow all sorts of crops. They grow grapes in **vineyards** to make wine. They grow lemons, oranges and olives for olive oil. The flat land of the plateau is good for growing wheat and barley. They keep sheep and goats for milk and meat. They keep pigs too.

14

Spain is famous for making a special sort of wine called sherry.

HELPING CROPS GROW

The long dry summers are a problem for farmers in most of Spain. Sometimes there is not enough rain for the crops even in the winter. This is a problem the Moors faced too, over 1000 years ago.

The answer to the problem, then and now, is **irrigation**. This is using water from rivers, **reservoirs** or underground. Ordinary farms use irrigation. So do the small farms that grow water-hungry vegetables, like tomatoes and melons.

A farmer checking his vines. He grows vegetables like sweetcorn and cabbages too.

LIFE ON A FARM

THE MERINO FAMILY

Chelo Merino lives in a flat in Marcilla in the north of Spain. She lives with her brother Enrique and her two boys; Javier (who is 19) and Manolo (who is 17).

The family and some friends in their flat in Marcilla.

The family own a farm near Marcilla. They keep bulls that are used for bullfighting and bull running, which are popular sports in Spain. The bulls have to be fed special food to make them strong. They can be dangerous. Chelo's husband was killed by a bull a few years ago.

There are 300 bulls on the farm. They eat grass and bean stalks three times a day to grow strong.

The bulls are very valuable. The vet often comes to check that they are well.

THE FAMILY'S DAY

The family all work on their farm. The boys have worked there since they were 12. Everyone has breakfast at 7 am and then goes to work on the farm. They work until 8.30 pm, with a break for lunch.

The family can get almost everything they need in the local shops.

MEALTIMES

The family eat all of their meals together. They go home to the village for lunch at about 2 pm. They have their evening meal after they have got back from the farm, at about 9 pm. They eat meat, rice, vegetables and fruit. They eat bread with almost every meal.

SPANISH SHOPS

Spain used to be a very poor country. People did not have a lot of money to spend. Now Spain is richer. One of the main reasons for this is the money made from **tourists**.

A supermarket in Barcelona. Supermarket shopping is quicker than shopping in small shops.

BIGGER SHOPS

One of the effects of people having more money to spend is that there are more shops that sell clothes, food and other **goods** to Spanish people and tourists.

Even the food shops are bigger. Now busy shoppers can buy bread, cheese, cakes, vegetables, tinned goods and meat in supermarkets, rather than going to lots of different small shops.

Street bars and stalls in Valencia. You can find stalls like these in towns and cities all over Spain.

LOCAL SHOPS

People can still buy things from local shops and markets, even in the cities. Lots of people prefer these shops to supermarkets. Fruit and vegetables in the market are often fresher, because they have come straight from local farms.

OPENING HOURS

Most shops open at 9.30 am, but some, especially bread shops, open earlier. Most shops close at about 2 pm. They stay closed for the hottest part of the day. They open again at about 4.30 pm and stay open until about 8 pm.

People in Spain, and many other hot countries, stop work to eat and rest in the early afternoon when it is very hot.

SPANISH FOOD

TRADITIONAL FOOD

There are lots of Spanish dishes that have been cooked to the same recipes for many years. They use foods that can be grown or caught locally. Paella uses seafood, meat, vegetables and rice. Some recipes are suited to the weather. Gaspacho is a cold, spicy vegetable soup. It makes a good lunch in hot weather.

These people are eating paella straight from the pan it was cooked in.

These **tourists** are having a cold drink in a shady bar.

TAPAS BARS

You can find tapas bars all over Spain. Tapas are small snacks, served with a drink. They are made from meat and vegetables. Each bar makes its own sort of tapas. Tapas stop people from getting hungry between a small breakfast and a late lunch, or between lunch and dinner.

21

MADE IN SPAIN

Spain sells **goods** to other countries, from food and drink to cars. Goods sold to other countries are called exports.

SOUVENIRS

Spain makes most of its money from **tourists**, who spend money in hotels and restaurants. They also buy **souvenirs** of their visit. Most of the lace and guitars made in Spain are sold to tourists.

These men are pouring Rioja wine into bottles. Wine is Spain's biggest export.

FACTORIES

There are many more factories in the cities and towns now than there were 30 years ago. They make clothes and cars. There are shipyards that build ships.

Spanish workers are paid lower wages than workers doing the same jobs in the rest of Europe, so people find it cheaper to set up factories here, or to send jobs to factories in Spain rather than having them done in their own country. Many of the books that are used in British schools are printed in Spain.

Ford, a foreign car company, has its Ka cars made in Spain, in Valencia.

About 2 million cars are made in Spain each year. That is one car every four minutes!

GETTING AROUND

Spain is improving its road, rail and sea travel because of the **tourist** industry. Airports are being modernized too. But there are still places with narrow dirt roads in the less-visited parts of Spain.

RAILWAYS

Madrid is the centre of the rail network. Fast trains run from there to all the big cities like Seville and Barcelona. The trains from the cities to smaller places are slower and run less often.

Seville railway station. Fast trains can go at 250 kilometres per hour.

Trams run on rail tracks in the road. They have their own routes and stopping places, just like buses.

The trams in Valencia run along the main roads.

ROADS

The road system in Spain spreads out from Madrid, just like the railways. Even so, it is faster to travel by train. The train takes about three hours to reach Seville from Madrid. It takes about six hours by car. Also, you have to pay to drive on some motorways.

The roads to the tourist resorts have been improved. They go to the edges of the resorts and then go around them, to keep the traffic moving.

SPORTS AND HOLIDAYS

Football is a very popular sport in Spain. People like to play it and watch it on the TV and at football grounds.

BULLFIGHTING

Spanish people and **tourists** both go to see bullfights. Bullfighting has gone on in Spain for hundreds of years. A **matador**, with a red cape, fights a bull.

The bull chases the matador, who teases it with his cape. When it is tired, he kills it – unless it gets him first.

The new holiday hotels are built tall and close together, to fit in as many tourists as possible.

TIME OFF

People like to relax in cafés and bars, or go for a walk in the cool of the evening.

HOLIDAYS

Not many Spanish people leave Spain for their holidays. Some of them go to the beaches on the **coast**. Some of them go to the countryside, visiting relatives, or go skiing in the mountains.

In some parts of Spain they play pelota, an old Spanish sport. You have to hit a ball against a wall until someone misses.

27

FESTIVALS AND ARTS

People in Jerez dressed up for a horse fair, another traditional celebration.

FESTIVALS

Festivals are called fiestas in Spain. Many fiestas are to do with religion. Most Spanish people are Roman Catholic.

Most towns have their own saint who has a special saint's day. On this day people say special prayers and parade through the streets singing and dancing. People who have been named after the saint are given presents.

SPECIAL DAYS

Some parades and feasts remember things that have happened in Spain in the past. People dress up and decorate the streets with flowers and lights.

FLAMENCO

The flamenco is a traditional Spanish **gypsy** dance. Dancers wear traditional clothes. The music is usually played on a guitar, sometimes with a singer, and gets faster and faster. The dancers go faster, too, stamping their feet and clicking their fingers.

People are dressed up as Moors and Christians for this parade in Seville, to remember when they fought to control Spain.

Gypsies first came to Spain over 500 years ago. They are proud of all their traditions, including flamenco dancing.

SPAIN FACTFILE

People

People from Spain are called Spaniards.

Capital city

The capital city is Madrid. Madrid is in the centre of Spain.

Largest cities

Madrid is the largest city with about 3 million people. The second largest is Barcelona and the third largest is Valencia.

Head of country

The head of Spain is a king but the country is run by a **government**.

Population

There are about 40 million people living in Spain.

Money

The money in Spain is called the peseta.

Language

People speak Spanish. Spanish is one of the most common languages in the world.

Education

Children have to go to school from the age of 6 to 16.

GLOSSARY

civil war when a country's people fight each other

coast where the land meets the sea

goods things people have made

government people who run the country. In Spain the government is elected (chosen) by the people.

gypsies travelling people who came from India, but have spread all over the world

irrigation watering the land

lava melted rock from below the Earth's surface

matador a bullfighter

national park an area of land that belongs to the government and is left wild

peninsula a piece of land with water almost all around it

plaza an open square in a town, often with shops around the edges

reservoirs lakes made by people to store water

Roman Empire the Romans were people who, from Rome in Italy, took over much of Europe and other parts of the world from 750BC to AD300

souvenir a thing that reminds someone of a place they have seen

tourist someone who visits a place on holiday

vineyards where grapes grow

volcano a mountain that sometimes throws out melted rock or ash

INDEX